THIS BOOK IS

. Mr. Warren. George. Ker~

THE WORLD'S MOST USELESS/~~SEXY~~/
~~LOVABLE~~/~~UGLY~~/~~HORRIBLE~~/~~SWEET~~/
~~ADORABLE~~/~~STUPID~~/CUTE/SCORPION

WITH ALL MY LOVE / ~~BEST WISHES~~/
~~YOURS IN DISGUST~~ Joanne . . x x . . . .

P.S. PLEASE TAKE NOTE OF PAGE(S)
. 5 , 30 , 53 . possessed by a devil .
HA HA

THE SCORPIO BOOK

A CORGI BOOK 0 552 12323 4

First publication in Great Britain
PRINTING HISTORY
Corgi edition published 1983
Corgi edition reissued 1984
Corgi edition reprinted 1985

Corgi Books are published by Transworld Publishers Ltd.,
Century House, 61-63 Uxbridge Road, Ealing, London W5 5SA,
in Australia by Transworld Publishers (Aust.) Pty. Ltd.,
26 Harley Crescent, Condell Park, NSW 2200, and in New Zealand
by Transworld Publishers (N.Z.) Ltd., Cnr. Moselle and
Waipareira Avenues, Henderson, Auckland.

Made and printed in Great Britain by the
Guernsey Press Co. Ltd., Guernsey, Channel Islands.

THE SCORPIO BOOK

BY IAN HEATH

SCORPIO

OCTOBER 23 – NOVEMBER 22

EIGHTH SIGN OF THE ZODIAC
SYMBOL : THE SCORPION
RULING PLANET : MARS
COLOURS : SCARLET, YELLOW
GEM : RUBY
NUMBER : NINE
DAY : TUESDAY
METAL : STEEL
FLOWER : ORCHID

ZZZZZZZZZZ

The SCORPION at work.................

.........CAN BE PUSHY.................

..... WILL TOIL ALL HOURS ....

..... IS JEALOUS OF COLLEAGUES....

...LOVES DEALING WITH THE PUBLIC.....

.....SLIGHTLY DEVIOUS.............

......VERY IMAGINATIVE...........

..... A PROBLEM SOLVER............

...... IS ALWAYS RIGHT ....

.... AND CANNOT SIT STILL.

.........A CHAUFFEUR...............

.........HAIR SPECIALIST.............

.... CONDUCTOR ....

.... WOODWORM CONTROLLER ....

.........ELECTRICIAN.................

..........PLUMBER..............

...... OR TRAVEL AGENT.

..... IS A KEEN GARDENER ....

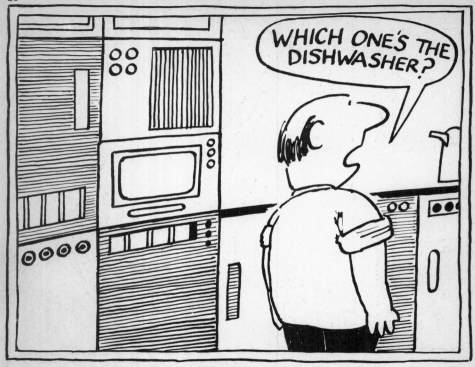

.... LOVES GADGETS..............

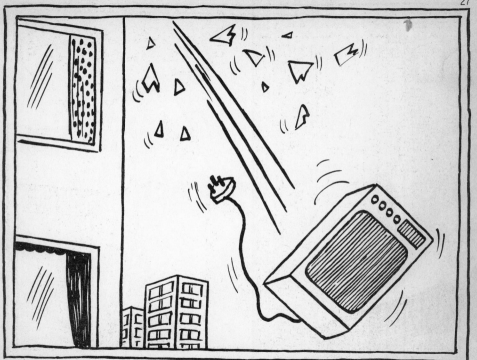

...... HATES TELEVISION..........

...HAS MANY INDOOR PLANTS....

..... SPENDS HOURS ON 'PHONE ....

......IS A LATE RISER...............

...... BAKES OWN BREAD..........

......ENJOYS BUILDING SHELVES......

......WALKING THE DOG..............

.....AND PROTECTS HIS (HER) PRIVACY.

.........CASUAL CLOTHES.............

.... BEING WARM ....

......SWIMMING......................

.....EXPENSIVE RESTAURANTS.....

.......TINNED RASPBERRIES..........

.... AND THUNDERSTORMS.

The
SCORPION
dislikes..................

..... PHONE-IN PROGRAMMES........

. . . . .GRAVY. . . . .

.......CIGAR SMOKE.................

.... BUSINESS MEETINGS............

BORES

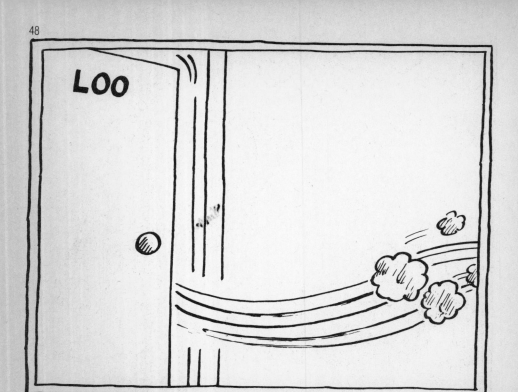

.... AND BAKED BEANS.

The SCORPION in love...............

.....ATTRACTS ATTENTION..........

.... IS SUPER-SEXY.................

......HAS MAGNETISM...............

.......IS POSSESSIVE...............

.... TELLS THE TRUTH.............

... HAS HIGH STANDARDS ....

...... DOESN'T HOLD BACK..........

..... CAN BE VERY JEALOUS........

.... HAS SEVERAL LOVERS........

... AND IS PASSIONATE.

SCORPIO
AND PARTNER
HEART RATINGS

♥♥♥♥♥ WOWEE!!
♥♥♥♥ GREAT, BUT NOT 'IT'
♥♥♥ O.K. — COULD BE FUN
♥♥ FORGET IT
♥ RUN THE OTHER WAY — FAST!

PISCES CANCER

SAGITTARIUS CAPRICORN
VIRGO LIBRA

AQUARIUS SCORPIO TAURUS

LEO ARIES

GEMINI

SCORPIO PEOPLE

PABLO PICASSO: GOLDIE HAWN
CHARLES DE GAULLE: VIVIEN LEIGH
THEODORE ROOSEVELT: DIANA DORS
BURT LANCASTER: RICHARD BURTON
H.R.H. PRINCESS GRACE OF MONACO

PRINCE CHARLES: DYLAN THOMAS
GARY PLAYER: KEN ROSEWALL
LESTER PIGGOTT: LEON TROTSKY
ROBERT KENNEDY: CHAD VARAH
MARIE CURIE: FRANKENSTEIN
ART GARFUNKEL: LOUIS MALLE
MARIE ANTOINETTE: ALAIN DELON
KATHERINE HEPBURN: PETER COOK
ROCK HUDSON: INDIRA GANDHI
PETULA CLARK: RAY CONNIFF
ALISTAIR COOK: TATUM O'NEAL